PIANO • VOCAL • GUITAR

A D E L E 30

ISBN: 978-1-70515-812-8

Visit Hal Leonard Online at
www.halleonard.com

Contact us:
Hal Leonard
7777 West Bluemound Road
Milwaukee, WI 53213
Email: info@halleonard.com

In Europe, contact:
Hal Leonard Europe Limited
42 Wigmore Street
Marylebone, London, W1U 2RY
Email: info@halleonardeurope.com

In Australia, contact:
Hal Leonard Australia Pty. Ltd.
4 Lentara Court
Cheltenham, Victoria, 3192 Australia
Email: info@halleonard.com.au

STRANGERS BY NATURE

WORDS AND MUSIC BY ADELE ADKINS AND LUDWIG GORANSSON

Lyrics:

I'll ___ be tak-ing flow-ers to the cem-e-ter-y of my heart,

for all of my lov-ers in the pres-ent and in the dark.

Ev-'ry an-ni-ver-sa-ry I'll pay re-spects and say I'm sor-ry,

some-day ____ I'll learn ____ to nur-ture what I've done.

Ooh, _____ mmm, _____ mmm, _____

mmm, _____ mmm, _____

_____ ooh. _____ (Spoken:) Alright then, I'm ready.

7

EASY ON ME

WORDS AND MUSIC BY ADELE ADKINS AND GREG KURSTIN

si - lence, ba - by, let me in. Go ea - sy on me, ba - by, I was still a child, did-n't get the chance to feel the world a - round me. I had no time to choose what I chose to do, so go ea - sy on me.

I had _____ good _ in - ten - tions _____ and the high - est _____

D.S. al Coda

_____ hopes _____ but I know right now _____ it pro-b'ly does-n't e-ven show. _____ Go

CODA

_____ to do, _____ so go ea - sy _____ on _____ me.

MY LITTLE LOVE

WORDS AND MUSIC BY ADELE ADKINS AND GREG KURSTIN

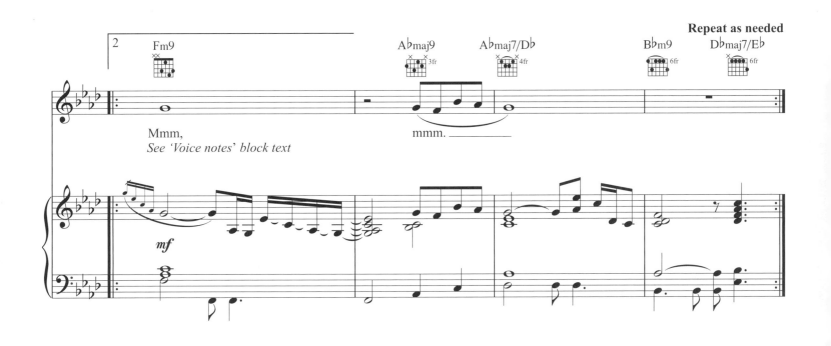

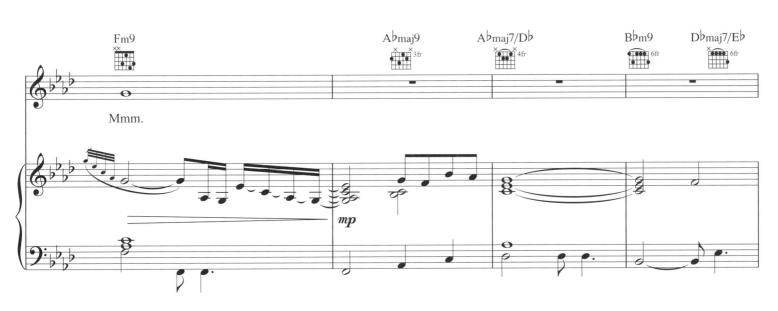

Voice notes

I'm having a bad day, I'm having a very anxious day

I feel very paranoid, I feel very stressed

Um, I have a hangover

Which never helps, but

I feel like today is the first day

Since I left him that I feel lonely

And I never feel lonely,

I love being on my own

I always preferred being on my own than being with people

And I feel like maybe I've been, like, overcompensating

Being out and stuff like that to keep my mind off of it

And I feel like today I'm home, and I wanna be at home I just wanna watch TV

And curl up in a ball and

Be in my sweats and stuff like that, I just feel really lonely

I feel a bit frightened that I might feel like this a lot

CRY YOUR HEART OUT

WORDS AND MUSIC BY ADELE ADKINS AND GREG KURSTIN

go _____ at your own _____ pace. When I _____ pace.

All _____ love is de - vout, no feel-ing is a waste, but give it to your-self now, be - fore _ it's too

late. In the end it's just you, stop drown-ing in wait, ___ your love is use - less with-out it.

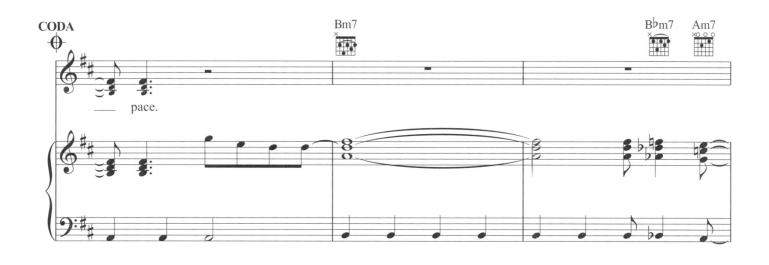

pace.

OH MY GOD

WORDS AND MUSIC BY ADELE ADKINS AND GREG KURSTIN

*Originally recorded a half step lower
Vocal line originally recorded one octave lower

Wish that I would let you break my walls _____ but I'm still spin -
I'm a fool, but they all think I'm blind, _____ I'd rath - er be __

- ning out of con - trol from the fall. _____
__ a fool than leave my - self be - hind. _____

Boy, you give good love, I won't lie, _____ it's what keeps me com -
I don't have to ex - plain my - self to you, _____ I am a grown __

- ing back e - ven though I'm ter - ri - fied. _____
__ wom - an and I do what I want to do. _____

all the peo - ple in the world, _ what _ is the _ like - li - hood of jump - ing

out of my life and in - to yours? ___ May - be, ba - by, I'm just los - ing my mind

'cause this is trou - ble, but it feels right, tee - t'ring on the edge of Heav - en and Hell,

To Coda ⊕ | 1

it's a bat - tle that I can - not ___ fight. _

31

CAN I GET IT

WORDS AND MUSIC BY ADELE ADKINS, SHELLBACK AND MAX MARTIN

I have prom-ised I ____ will love you till ____ the end of time, ____

through it all, the good, _ the bad, the ug - ly, and di - vine. ____

I will be the mel - o - dy, the rhy - thm, and your rhyme, ____

all I want is for _ you to be mine. ____ So can I get it right

now? _____

Can I get it right

now? _____

(Can I get it?) ___ Can I get it right

now? _____

Can I get it right

now? _____

Let me, let me just come and get it.

(Can I get it?) ___

You

When will you

run with me, ___ like I know you want to? (Like __ you want to, __

like __ you want.) You're the ___ one for me ___ and I'm count-ing on you

I DRINK WINE

WORDS AND MUSIC BY ADELE ADKINS AND GREG KURSTIN

How can one be-come so bound-ed by choic-es that some-bod-y _____ else makes? How come we've both

learn to get o - ver ___ my - self,

stop try - ing to be ___ some - bod - y else. ___

{ Oh, I just want to love you, love you ___ for free. ___
So we can love you, each oth - er for ___

___ free.

Ev - 'ry - bod - y wants some - thing,
Ev - 'ry - bod - y wants some - thing from ___ me, }

we're both none the wis - er.

Spoken: The only regret I have,

I wish that it was just at a different time. A most turbulent

period of my life.

Why would I put that on you?

That's just, like, a very heavy thing to have to talk about

but because of that

period of time,

even though it was so much fun,

I didn't get to go on and make new

memories with him,

there was just memories in a big storm.

ALL NIGHT PARKING
(INTERLUDE)

WORDS AND MUSIC BY ADELE ADKINS AND ERROLL GARNER

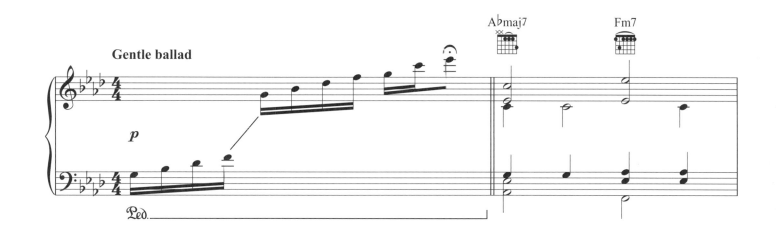

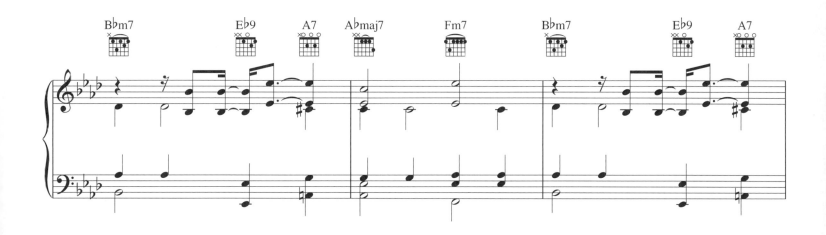

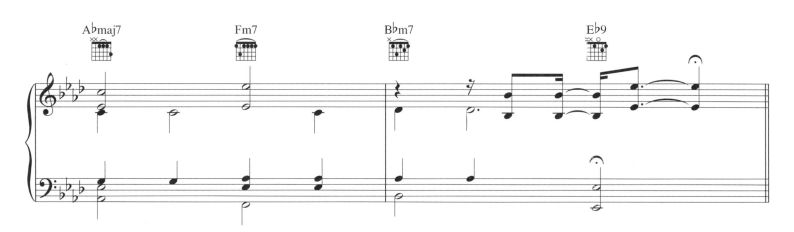

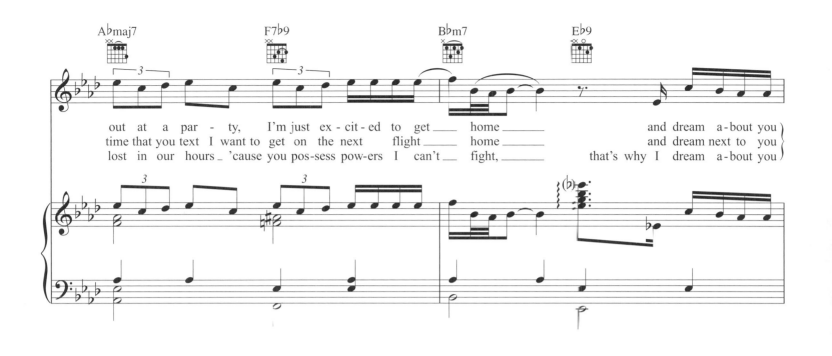

out at a par - ty, I'm just ex - cit - ed to get ____ home ____ and dream a - bout you
time that you text I want to get on the next flight ____ home ____ and dream next to you
lost in our hours _ 'cause you pos - sess pow - ers I can't ____ fight, ____ that's why I dream a - bout you

all ___ night long. ___

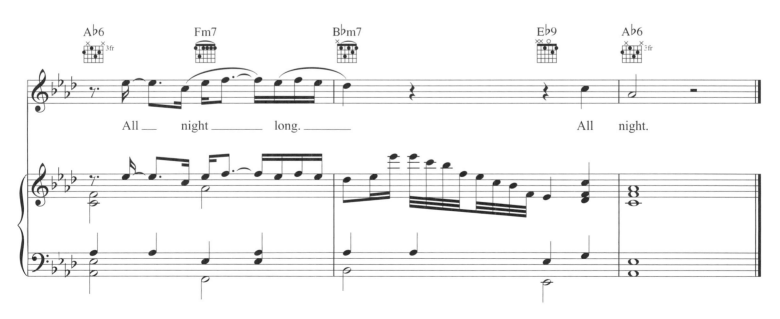

All ___ night ____ long. ____ All night.

WOMAN LIKE ME

WORDS AND MUSIC BY ADELE ADKINS AND DEAN JOSIAH COVER

D.S. al Coda

CODA

Cmaj7

A wom-an like ___ me. ___

B7+   Em9

Com-pla-cen - cy   is the
                                (Wom - an ___ like

Cmaj7

worst   trait to have,   are you cra - zy?
me.)   (Wom - an ___ like

You ain't

B7+   Em9

ev - er had, _   ain't ev - er had a wom-an like ___ me.
me.)   It is

60

HOLD ON

WORDS AND MUSIC BY ADELE ADKINS AND DEAN JOSIAH COVER

TO BE LOVED

WORDS AND MUSIC BY ADELE ADKINS AND TOBIAS JESSO

LOVE IS A GAME

WORDS AND MUSIC BY ADELE ADKINS AND DEAN JOSIAH COVER

Originally recorded a half step higher

self - in - flict _____   that   pain. _____

DISCOVER MORE ADELE SHEET MUSIC

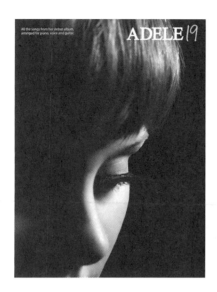

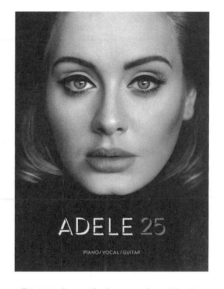

PIANO, VOCAL, GUITAR
HL00307038

EASY PIANO
HL00307319

PIANO, VOCAL, GUITAR
HL00307247

EASY PIANO
HL00307320

VERY EASY PIANO:
HL00100321

PIANO, VOCAL, GUITAR
HL00155393

EASY PIANO
HL00155394

EASY GUITAR
HL00156221

UKULELE
HL00156811

PIANO PLAYALONG:
HL00156222

HL14060430

HL00155395

HL14060414